Jan. 7, 2008

Policy Debate

Cynthia Burgett

The National Forensic League

Library of Public Speaking and Debate

rosen publishing's
rosen
central®

New York

To my mother, who has made possible the crazy life of a debate coach; to Sarah Thomas,
without whom I wouldn't have made it through the first year of coaching; to all of my
debate coaches, who have mentored me and helped me along the way; and to my students.

Published in 2007 by The Rosen Publishing Group, Inc.
29 East 21st Street, New York, NY 10010

First Edition

Library of Congress Cataloging-in-Publication Data

Burgett, Cynthia.
  Policy debate / Cynthia Burgett.
      p. cm. — (The National Forensic League library of public speaking and debate)
  Includes index.
  ISBN-10: 1-4042-1024-5 (lib. bdg.)
  ISBN-13: 978-1-4042-1024-0
  1. Debates and debating—Juvenile literature. 2. Forensics (Public speaking)—
Juvenile literature. 3. Policy sciences—Juvenile literature. I. National Forensic
League (U.S.) II. Title.
  PN4181.B78 2007
  808.53—dc22

Manufactured in the United States of America

The National Forensic League Honor Society promotes secondary school speech and debate activities and interscholastic competition as a means to develop a student's lifelong skills and values, as well as the public's awareness of the value of speech, debate, and communication education.

The organization serves as the central agent for coordination and facilitation of

- heightened public awareness of the value of speech communication skills;
- development of educational initiatives for student and teacher training;
- excellence in interscholastic competition;
- the promotion of honor society ideals.

As an organization, the National Forensic League embraces diversity, interconnection, and visionary leadership. The National Forensic League empowers students to become effective communicators, ethical individuals, critical thinkers, and leaders in a democratic society.

To learn more about starting a National Forensic League or National Junior Forensic League program at the middle or high school level or to locate more resources on speech and/or debate, please contact National Forensic League, 125 Watson Street, Ripon, WI 54971, (920) 748-6206, or visit our Web site at **www.nflonline.org**.

Contents

Chapter 1

What Is Policy Debate?

Policy debate (also called cross-examination debate) is a form of speech competition in which two teams—each with two members—debate the advantages and weaknesses of national policy issues. The issue to be ~~debated, known as~~ the "resolution," remains the same throughout the school year. The team that wants the resolution to be made into law is called the "affirmative." The team that opposes the resolution is called the "negative." In most states, a team will debate both for the resolution (affirmative) and against it (negative) in alternating rounds. The members of each side speak according to a schedule and question each other in cross-examination periods. At the end of the tournament, a judge decides which side was more persuasive and hands a written ballot to the tournament tab room, which is where the ballots are compared and a winner is determined. The best teams at the tournament enter elimination periods—periods during which winners from previous rounds are paired together for a new round of debating.

Siege Mentality

A policy debate can be compared to an attack on a fort. The affirmative builds a fort, and the negative attacks it. Let's consider the following situation: Your mother believes that you should clean up your room. Your mother is the affirmative, you are the negative, and your dad is the judge.

The affirmative "fort" has two parts: the affirmative case and the plan. If the affirmative loses either part, then the enemy—or the negative—can capture the fort and win the debate. Your mother presents the affirmative case, which gives reasons why you should clean your room. Your mother shows the judge your room with the fungi climbing the walls and the rats she found under your bed. Next, she presents the plan, which is how the action is to be put into effect: She says she will pull out one of your fingernails each hour until the job is done.

It is the responsibility of the negative to attack the fort established by the affirmative by responding specifically to what the affirmative said. You present your negative case to the judge and explain that the fungi on the walls have been carefully cultivated for sale to a penicillin factory. The rats are part of your plan to save your father money by having his taxes cut when your room is declared a wildlife refuge. Next, you refute the affirmative plan by saying that since your mother's nagging has reduced you to chewing your fingernails, there is not enough left to torture you with. Notice that the negative is responding directly to what the affirmative has said. This is the duty of the negative—to create clash.

Because I Said So!

What if the affirmative does not establish a solid fort for the negative to attack? What if your mother's affirmative case were the words "Because I said so"? This type of argument cannot be debated. The negative has nothing to attack. In an actual debate, an affirmative who says very little usually loses the debate. The affirmative must present a prima facie (PRY-muh FAY-shuh) case. This means that the affirmative case and plan seem reasonable to the judge and give

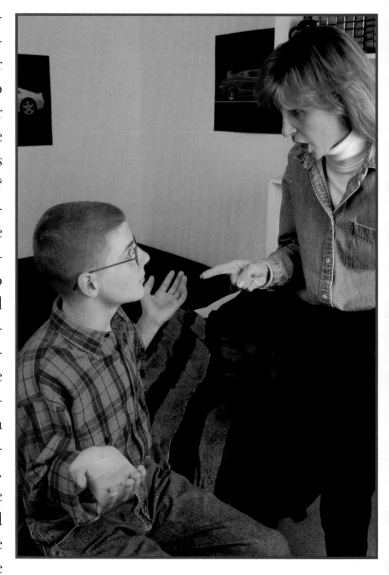

the negative something to discuss. If the affirmative fails the prima facie test, the negative wins the debate. This is called "negative presumption."

Affimative

You say that your mother makes you clean your room even though you clearly won the debate? This is because you are having a fight and not a debate. The people with the loudest voices, biggest muscles, or most authority usually win fights. The most persuasive people win debates. When a judge votes affirmative, the affirmative side has persuaded the judge that the proposed plan should be put into effect. If the judge votes negative, they were not persuaded that the affirmative proposal was a good one. To avoid having debates turn into fights, the arrangement for debate is divided so that each side has an equal amount of time.

Taking Turns

Unlike arguments with your mother, policy debates follow a concrete series of steps. These steps are always the same and are designed to make the debate fair for both sides. They also insure that the debate does not go on too long. Given the chance, many debaters would argue their case for more than 8 minutes. You should be able to state your case and give plenty of evidence in the time permitted.

The format of a policy debate is demonstrated on page 10. This chart explains the turns that the affirmative and negative sides must take during a typical debate. It also indicates the amount of time each speaker is allowed. Cross-examination periods are much shorter than the time allowed to present constructives. All debaters are allowed 5 minutes each at the end of the debate for rebuttal. You will find more information about this format later in the book.

Standard Policy or Cross-Examination Debate Schedule

First Affirmative Constructive (1AC) — 8 minutes

    Second Negative Cross-Examines First Affirmative — 3 minutes

First Negative Constructive (1NC) — 8 minutes

    First Affirmative Cross-Examines First Negative — 3 minutes

Second Affirmative Constructive (2AC) — 8 minutes

    First Negative Cross-Examines Second Affirmative — 3 minutes

Second Negative Constructive (2NC) — 8 minutes

    Second Affirmative Cross-Examines Second Negative — 3 minutes

First Negative Rebuttal (1NR) — 5 minutes

First Affirmative Rebuttal (1AR) — 5 minutes

Second Negative Rebuttal (2NR) — 5 minutes

Second Affirmative Rebuttal (2AR) — 5 minutes

I'm So Confused!

At first, policy debate may seem confusing. That's okay. When you go to your first tournament, you may still be dazed by all the information you have to juggle to be a good debater. Fear not! Eventually, all this will make perfect sense to you. Don't give up, and don't be afraid to ask questions.

Chapter 2

The Stock Issues

Just like the debate itself, preparing for a debate is a highly structured process. Before you can debate a topic, there are some basic things you need to understand regarding that topic. Stock issues are a starting point for debate preparation. They create focal points for both the affirmative and the negative teams.

Generally, there are five stock issues. Significance demonstrates there is a problem to begin with. Inherency proves there is nothing being done at present to fix the problem. Solvency provides a plan to fix the problem. Advantage is the result you hope to achieve by meeting the previous three issues. And topicality demonstrates that the proposed plan does in fact support the initial resolution. When all these pieces fall into place, it is said that the affirmative has met the burden of proof.

Significance: What's the Problem?

The first question you need to ask about an issue is this: Is there a problem? If there isn't a problem, then there isn't a reason to change the way things are. In debate, this issue is called "significance."

Significance can be divided into two parts. First, you must show that the problem has magnitude, or size (how many people does the problem affect?). Second, you must show that the problem has some kind of impact, or harm (what bad things happen as a result of the way things are currently done?).

If you are trying to prove that we should increase the number of people serving in the military, then you first need to show why we should do that. In a May 10, 2005, article on the MSNBC Web site, Jim Miklaszewski states that the U.S. Army missed its recruiting goal for the third month in a row. They were short by almost 2,800 recruits, or roughly 42 percent of the target. This shows the magnitude of the problem. When the army falls short of its recruiting goals, they are less ready to fight wars and protect the country. Soldiers have to do longer tours of duty, and more of the reserves and state National Guards have to serve abroad. This means the National Guard is less prepared to respond to crises at home, such as Hurricane Katrina. These points highlight the impact of the problem.

Inherency

Once you have proven there is a problem with the way things are being done in the present system (also called the status quo), you must show there is an actual reason why nothing (or nothing effective) is being done to solve that problem. This stock issue is called "inherency" or an "inherent barrier."

In the example of the low number of recruits, part of

the inherency is that sometimes the military doesn't accept recruits who might be fit to serve and who want to serve. The laws that govern recruitment only allow for a limited number of people who haven't graduated from high school. People who are openly homosexual aren't allowed to serve in the military. Women aren't allowed to serve in combat positions. All of these rules may make it harder for the army to recruit new members; it is an inherent barrier to fixing the recruitment problem.

Solvency: I Have a Great Plan!

So far, you have explained the problem (significance) and the barriers to fixing that problem (inherency). Now everyone wants to know what you are going to do to solve the problem. "Solvency" is a stock issue in which a number of critical debate ideas come into play. First, you must have a plan that can be used to solve the problem. Second, the problem must be solved by an actor. The actor is usually the U.S. government.

The plan must specify what exactly you want to do to solve the problem. It should make sure that the inherent barrier is eliminated (laws repealed, attitudes changed, and so forth), and it should provide for funding, enforcement, and administration of the plan. (Usually you'll hear the words "through normal means" for this part of the plan.) Here's an example using the recruitment topic:

> **PLAN:** The U.S. government will substantially increase the number of people serving in the armed forces by enacting the Rangel-Hollings Bill. All funding, enforcement, and administration will be through normal means. The affirmative team reserves the right to clarify intent.

If this were your plan, you would need to be able to explain the Rangel-Hollings Bill. It requires all citizens between the ages of 18 and 26 to serve in either a military or a civilian capacity for a period of 2 years. College attendance would no longer be a legitimate reason to defer service. High school students would be able to defer only until their twentieth birthday or the completion of their high school diploma. You would also need to explain that "normal means" would include using the selective service process that was used in the last draft (for the Vietnam War) or some other mechanism to make your plan work smoothly. No matter what you choose, you should be able to explain your plan in detail if you are asked in cross-examination.

A Magic Wand

Carrying out a plan introduces an interesting concept called "fiat." Fiat is the affirmative's "magic wand." It is their right to assume that their plan will be

adopted by the federal government—that Congress would vote for it, the president would sign any necessary bills, and the Supreme Court would not overturn it. This assumption exists so that the debate centers on whether or not the plan is a good idea, rather than whether our government would actually make it into a law.

For instance, if your plan was to bring back the draft, there's a chance Congress wouldn't pass the proposal. Even if Congress passed it, the president would likely veto it, since the majority of Americans do not support the idea of being drafted or having their children and grandchildren drafted. With fiat, you don't have to worry about what Congress or the president would do. However, you will still have to answer arguments about how the public would perceive your plan.

Prove It!

Despite the magical properties of fiat, solvency requires evidence. You must do research and have evidence to show that your plan will work. Find out what other qualified, educated people think ought to be done about the issue. Write your plan so that it follows what the experts say. Then you can read evidence from them to support your plan.

Advantage

When these stock issues—significance, inherency, and solvency—come together, then you should have multiple advantages to demonstrate the benefits of your plan. Some people consider advantages a stock issue all by themselves. If your plan doesn't solve the problem you outlined in the significance portion of your case, it may be hard to show you have any advantages at all. Ultimately, it may be hard to win the debate.

Enacting the plan that reinstitutes the draft could claim to have numerous advantages, such as making the military stronger and decreasing racism (since everyone would have to serve together, regardless of race). Once you research a plan and find someone with a proposal, that someone will likely have many good reasons (advantages) for supporting the plan.

Topicality: A Rule of Debate

The final stock issue of policy debating—"topicality"—asks the question: Does the affirmative plan directly support the resolution? Topicality insures that the affirmative offers a fair plan to which the negative can respond with evidence. If fiat is the affirmative team's "magic wand," topicality is the negative team's "suit of armor."

The negative team has to be prepared to debate any possible affirmative plan that falls within the resolution—which is a huge number of possible plans. They can't be sure what plan the affirmative team will decide to argue until the round begins. It might be one that expands AmeriCorps, or it might be one that brings back the draft. The negative can't just assume that all affirmative teams will argue to bring back the draft. But what if the affirmative plan states that the U.S. government should disarm all of its nuclear weapons? While that might be a good idea, it doesn't really support the national service resolution, and it isn't something the negative team would have anticipated as a possible plan. Therefore, it wouldn't be a fair fight for the negative, since they would have no evidence. After appealing to the judge about the nontopicality of the plan, the negative team would hope to win the debate on that basis.

Chapter 3

Arguments, Evidence, and Researching

In order to be successful in policy debate, you need to be able to make winning arguments that your judge will believe. An effective argument consists of two elements. A claim is a statement that expresses what the affirmative believes to be true. The proof or evidence is the information that the affirmative supplies to make the judge believe that their claim is true.

When you make a claim, you need to have sufficient proof to back it up. For instance, you could claim that you are the best singer in school. If you don't have the pipes to prove it, however, your argument is not very believable.

In a policy debate, you are going to be making many claims. Making the claim alone, however, will not be enough to win a debate. Without believable proof or evidence, the judge probably won't side with you. If your opponent's evidence is more believable than yours, chances are they will win the debate.

Evidence

There are four types of evidence you can use to prove your claim. A personal observation can be good, but it's generally a weak type of proof. The best types of evidence are expert testimony, the results of a study, and empirical examples (such as: this was done before, and the result was . . .). Evidence is usually found in magazines, newspapers, journals, and books.

Gathering evidence can mean a lot of time at the library and in front of the computer, but it is necessary when constructing a strong, effective argument.

Debaters commonly call organized evidence "cards." This is because many years ago evidence was pasted onto note cards. Today, evidence is usually organized on full sheets of paper, often with two or three "cards" per sheet. A card contains three elements: the tag (the summary of the argument), the citation or cite (the source of the evidence), and the body (the actual quoted evidence). Researching and organizing information to use in debate is called "cutting cards."

TAG →

CITE

BODY

CLAIM: Mandatory national service is slavery.

EVIDENCE: Melinda Bass, (Ph.D. Dissertation, Department of Politics, Brandeis University), THE POLITICS AND "CIVICS" OF NATIONAL SERVICE, August 4, 1966.

No single issue inflames the passions of national service opponents more than the thought that it may become obligatory. At best, they believe that such a requirement would epitomize an oxymoron—"forced volunteerism"—or be a "tax on time"; at worst, it would represent "indentured servitude" or "slavery," in violation of both morality and the Thirteenth Amendment.

Fact Finders

The first step to debating using quality evidence is to actually find quality evidence. The best place to look is at a library or on respected computer databases and Web sites. (Avoid Web sites that are not research bases or recognized organizations.) Read articles about the topic, and search for facts that help you prove the argument you want to make. When you go to the library, spend your time finding and copying information you think will be useful. Photocopy or print those articles and write notes all over them! Then bring them home or to school where you can "cut" your evidence.

Some people in the policy debate community research each year's topic and assemble books and electronic evidence files you can buy. Much of this evidence is already "cut" into "card" form. This may save you time, but it won't help you improve as a debater. Discovering for yourself what authors intended to say will ultimately make you a better debater.

Cutting Evidence

When you first start looking at articles, trying to decide what is valuable evidence can be overwhelming. However, you will begin to recognize "cards" as you do more "card cutting." Here are some simple guidelines for cutting evidence to use in debate:

- When in doubt, mark the card and cut it. You can always get rid of it later if it's not any good, but sometimes it's hard to go back and find something you know you read but failed to cut.
- When in doubt, cut it long. You can always make it shorter later. But if you didn't get it all the first time, again, it's hard to go back and find the information you did not record.
- Cut for both the affirmative and negative sides. Good

21

debaters know what the other side will say against them and anticipate arguments. Also, you may need the cards you're cutting in rounds when you're on the other side.

- Try to cut evidence that gives reasons for the author's opinion. One-sentence cards that don't have any analysis aren't as persuasive as cards that have good reasons for the author's opinion.
- When cutting cards, don't alter sentences or cut out the middle of an article to save time. This can change the author's meaning. Consider this sentence: It is . . . necessary for Congress to fund social programs (omitted: neither practical nor). The omitted words dramatically change the sentence meaning. In competition, you can just read parts of the evidence, but all of it must be available if the other team asks to see your evidence.
- As you read articles, make notes in the margin about the claim you think the evidence makes. In debate, we call these tags. By tagging your cards as you read, you are saving yourself time later when you actually cut the evidence off the printout or photocopy.
- Never fake evidence or alter what an author wrote. For cheating, you will usually be disqualified or even kicked off your squad.

Citing Evidence

It is especially important that you have a citation, or cite, for every piece of evidence you cut from an article. Remember, individual "cards" may be in different parts of your files, so you should put a citation on every single card.

A complete citation should contain the following information:

- The author's full name (at least first and last)
- The author's qualifications (in parentheses)
- The title of the publication (usually written in capital letters)
- The full date of publication, if available (month/day/year)
- URL of your source for online databases

Typing citations can seem like a lot of work, but you can use a computer to type the citation once and then copy it many times before printing and attaching each individual citation to a cut piece of evidence. Just remember one important thing: don't leave the library, Web site, or database before you get all the information you'll need for the citation.

Example Citations

journal article:

> P. Andrew Achilles (prof. of history, Carnegie Mellon University), MODERN VOLUNTEERISM, Jan 29, 2002.

article on a research database:

> P. Andrew Achilles (prof. of history, Carnegie Mellon University), MODERN VOLUNTEERISM, Jan 29, 2002, Lexis-Nexis. Date of access: March 24, 2006.

Web page on the Internet:

> P. Andrew Achilles (prof. of history, Carnegie Mellon University), MODERN VOLUNTEERISM, Jan 29, 2002, Cato Institute, www.cato.org. Date of access: March 24, 2006.

Chapter 4

Writing an Affirmative Case

If you understand stock issues and cutting evidence, you are ready for a debate. However, the debate can't begin unless the affirmative team is ready to read the first affirmative constructive (1AC). Everyone else will be responding to these arguments with speeches made, in part, "on the spot." The 1AC is the speech that should be ready to go before you even go to the tournament.

The 1AC has three purposes. First, it should tell a clear, persuasive story. It should have an introduction, transitions, and clear explanations. If the story isn't clear and persuasive to the judge from the beginning of the round, it will be difficult to win many affirmative rounds. Second, the 1AC has to meet the burden of proof, or fulfill the stock issues. Meeting your burden of proof is part of what will make the affirmative compelling. Third, the 1AC ought to be written with a strategy in mind for the rest of the round.

Organizing Your Evidence

You first need to choose an affirmative case that interests you, has evidence to prove the claims it makes, and is strategically sound. Each year, the resolution is written to be broad enough to encompass many possible affirmatives, so you have many affirmative case choices. For 2007, Jeff Jarman suggested in *The Forensic Quarterly* some affirmatives on national service, including the following:

- expanding AmeriCorps as suggested by Senator John Kerry in the 2004 presidential campaign
- bringing back funding for the National Civilian Community Corps
- passing the Call to Service Act of 2001
- increasing financial aid and benefits to those who perform national service in AmeriCorps, Senior Corps, or Citizen Corps
- increasing the number of individuals allowed to serve in the Peace Corps
- bringing back the draft
- expanding the citizen soldier program, which allows for a shorter term of active duty
- changing the federal work-study program to change the number of students allowed to serve in work study or increase the amount of community (as opposed to university) service that must be done for work study
- expanding the age requirements for those serving in Senior Corps (Foster Grandparents, the Senior Companion program, and Retired and Senior Volunteer Program)
- instituting new service learning projects through Learn and Serve America

Once you have decided on a case area, you need to gather evidence to fulfill your affirmative burden of proof, or the stock issues. If you sort your evidence into stock issues piles—significance, inherency, solvency, advantages—it will help you organize your 1AC. The 1AC allows some flexibility in terms of how the evidence is structured. In some places, the 1AC is structured as a formal outline; in other places, it isn't necessarily a formal outline, but it is certainly organized. Your coach will help you decide how to proceed.

Writing the 1AC

When you write your 1AC, you will use chunks of information called "observations," or "contentions," to present your evidence. Your first two observations should be your significance evidence and your inherency evidence. Your story will be organized for the judge in one of two ways:

1. Inherency, then significance:
   - Observation 1: The status quo has a policy that is misguided (inherency).
   - Observation 2: Following that policy has led to bad things (significance).

2. Significance, then inherency:
   - Observation 1: Things are bad now (significance).
   - Observation 2: The status quo is not able to make the bad situation better or has policies that keep things bad (inherency).

It doesn't really matter which issue you cover first, as long as your organization makes sense. It is common to have only one inherency card in the 1AC (although you can have more), but you will want to have more than one significance card in the 1AC if you want to be able to win rounds with your case.

Next, you want to write your plan. First, look carefully at the evidence you have for solvency. You will need to model your plan after what your solvency evidence says will work. You may have a cool and zany idea about what will solve the problem you set up in significance (let's give all teenagers brand-new cars if they do national service), but if you don't have evidence to support that idea, you won't win many rounds. Be practical and find authors who say exactly what they think should be done, and then write your plan to match those authors' ideas.

Once you are satisfied with your plan, include your solvency and advantage observations. These are the benefits of carrying out your plan. In general, your 1AC should have roughly eight to fifteen pieces of evidence. If you are in a debate where very fast speaking is normal, you might want more in the 1AC, but don't put so much evidence in the 1AC that you can't get through it in 8 minutes. You aren't allowed to keep reading after the 8 minutes are up!

Also, don't use every piece of evidence you have in the 1AC. A competent negative team will have a thing or two to say about your affirmative, and you will want additional evidence to strengthen your case in the 2AC and rebuttals. Rereading the evidence you presented in the 1AC won't strengthen your point—it just repeats it. And if the negative team had a great argument against it, repetition won't be enough for you to win. When preparing, think about what you would say against your own 1AC if you were the negative, and then save some good evidence for the 2AC to answer those arguments.

Don't be afraid to edit and improve your case throughout your competitive season. Good debaters are always on the lookout for the most current cards to add to their affirmative files and for the best strategies and answers to negative arguments.

An Example 1AC

Here's an example of how a 1AC might be organized in outline form:

Observation 1: U.S. military forces are not sufficient now (significance).

  A. There are too few troops to cover operations in Iraq, Afghanistan, North Korea, Europe, and other world hot spots.

> Insert evidence here

  B. Recruitment efforts have fallen short for the past few years.

>Insert evidence here

  C. Troop shortages leave the United States open to attacks by hostile forces both at home and abroad.

>Insert evidence here

Observation 2: Current recruitment policies leave many able-bodied individuals unable to serve (inherency).

>Insert evidence here

PLAN: The U.S. federal government will substantially increase the number of persons serving in the armed forces by doing away with its Don't Ask, Don't Tell policy and its official stand on not allowing women in combat positions. The plan will be brought about by normal means. Affirmative reserves the right to clarify intent.

Observation 3: Solvency
  A. Allowing homosexuals to serve openly in the military will increase recruits.
    > Insert evidence here
  B. Doing away with the Don't Ask, Don't Tell policy will keep more soldiers in the military who currently risk being expelled because of their sexual orientation (homosexuality).
    > Insert evidence here
  C. If women were not restricted in the types of positions they were allowed, more would choose the military as a career.
    > Insert evidence here

Advantage 1: Sexism
  A. Allowing women and gays to serve openly decreases sexism and discrimination throughout society.
    > Insert evidence here
  B. Sexism and discrimination are social evils that must be erased.
    > Insert evidence here
  C. Any discrimination against minorities must always be rejected.
    > Insert evidence here

Advantage 2: Military readiness
  A. Increasing the number of soldiers serving in the military would increase the U.S. military's readiness.
    > Insert evidence here
  B. Readiness is the key to winning wars.
    > Insert evidence here
  C. Readiness is the best way to fight terrorism.
    > Insert evidence here

Chapter 5

Negative Arguments

So far, you've seen several examples of affirmative cases. Hopefully, you have been saying to yourself that there seems to be something wrong with some of those affirmative cases. This means you've been thinking like a member of the negative team.

During a policy debate tournament, you will be required to debate both sides of the resolution: affirmative and negative. Although you have one affirmative case, there are a good number of other possible cases that the other team may run. This means that your negative file will be much larger than your affirmative file. You need to spend time organizing your negative evidence so that you can find it quickly and efficiently. Scrambling around and searching for something to say makes you look less competent than the affirmative team, who had the 1AC ready to go.

Ready to Argue?

No matter how perfect an affirmative case may sound at first, there are always arguments that you can run against it. For some arguments, you will have a wide selection of evidence; for others, you may only be able to make observations about flaws you see. The arguments you will want to make are often already in your files. You shouldn't have to think these up on the spot. Look at the indexes you have for your negative evidence to help you decide what sorts of things you want to say about the flaws in the affirmative case. Be sure to make many different kinds of arguments in the debate round to increase your chances of winning.

What's the Problem? Arguing Significance

There are three ways a negative team can respond to the claims an affirmative team makes concerning significance. Attacking the claims of significance made by the affirmative doesn't often win a debate round all by itself, but it does help give weight to some of your other arguments, so don't be afraid to attack.

Let's say the affirmative team claims that the military isn't meeting its quotas for recruitment. There are three ways to attack the significance:

- <u>Direct denial</u>—You can say there isn't really a problem at all: The military has met its goals for recruitment. We have evidence to prove it.

- <u>Reduce the magnitude</u>—You can say the affirmative team is exaggerating the problem: Even if they aren't getting as many recruits as they had hoped, they don't need as many because advanced technology makes up for sheer numbers of soldiers.

- <u>Turn the impact</u>—You can say that what they claim is a bad thing is actually a good thing: It's a good thing we aren't making those recruitment goals. If we were, the president may want to invade hostile countries and that could result in World War III.

Inherency: Keep Back!

It is usually best to avoid saying anything against inherency claims made by the affirmative. Inherency claims state that the status quo is not currently doing the plan. As a negative, you should probably agree that the status quo is not doing the affirmative plan—because the affirmative plan isn't a good idea. If you argue that the status quo is already doing the affirmative, then it's hard to say later that doing the affirmative is a bad idea. It looks like you're contradicting yourself.

Can the Affirmative Solve the Problem?

There are three general types of solvency arguments. First, you can claim that the plan won't work because they've forgotten something important in their plan, such as funding or enforcement. This is called a "workability argument." For example, if the affirmative plan brings back the draft but doesn't establish draft boards or a process to draft people, it probably won't work very well.

A second reason the plan might not work is because people will ignore it and do what they've always done. This is called "circumvention." For instance, the affirmative team plans to increase the size of the military by repealing the Don't Ask, Don't Tell policy, and by allowing women into combat situations. The negative team can respond by saying this won't solve the problem that exists with recruiters and soldiers who discriminate against homosexuals and women regardless of government policy.

A third reason that the plan might not solve the problem is because it doesn't deal with all of the causes of the problem. Let's say the affirmative has a plan to increase the number of people serving in AmeriCorps by increasing scholarship money. You can point out that while money is a nice incentive, many people don't need scholarship money. Some will not go to college. Others don't want to do national service while they attend college because they need that time to study. In other words, money alone isn't the only reason people don't do national service. If the affirmative hasn't addressed all of the causes, they won't be able to solve the problem. This is called "alternate causality."

One of the best things a debater can do against solvency is "turn" it, or prove the affirmative case doesn't solve the problem, but makes it worse. Remember the affirmative case that said a small military is a bad thing? You could say that by making the military larger, the president may want to invade hostile counties. This could result in a decrease of new recruits, since most people aren't too eager to go to war.

Are They Topical?

What if the affirmative plan is to send astronauts to explore Mars? The affirmative is not establishing a policy to increase the number of people serving in the military in the resolution. They are not being topical. The round wouldn't be fair to you on the negative, since you came prepared to debate the resolution. If you look at an affirmative plan and it doesn't look topical, then topicality is an important argument you need to make in the first negative constructive (1NC).

Topicality arguments generally follow the same format. They begin with a definition of a word in the resolution. This is immediately followed by a description of how the affirmative's case violates the definition the negative has just provided. Next, the negative must explain to the judge why their definition of the word is a good one to use.

If all goes well, the negative team will convince the judge that their topicality argument is a "voting issue." This means that the judge agrees that the affirmative didn't directly address the topic raised by the resolution. This creates an unfair round for the negative. If this happens, the judge will not vote for the affirmative because it does not meet the topic. On the other hand, the judge could decide that the affirmative case is topical anyway and would have to look at other issues in the debate to decide the round.

Topicality arguments often boil down to a discussion of which team has the best definition and whether or not the affirmative team meets the definitions that have been given in the round.

By defining words in the resolution, you can show how

the affirmative doesn't meet their burden to be topical. For instance, if you define for the judges what "number of people" means and you show that all the affirmative does is increase the "number of dollars" given to a program, then you can show they fall outside of the topic. If the affirmative used Catholic Social Services to implement a plan, you would want to define what the federal government is and point out that the affirmative isn't using it, but instead is using a nongovernmental organization (NGO).

Disadvantages: The Big Gun

Another argument a negative can run is the disadvantage, which contends that if the affirmative plan is adopted, bad things are going to happen. At the end of the round, you will want to show that the disadvantages far outweigh the advantages to voting affirmative.

There are three main parts to a disadvantage argument. You must establish a link between the affirmative plan and the disadvantage that will follow. Next, you must show that the disadvantage will happen only if the judge votes for this affirmative. This is called "uniqueness." Finally, you must show what bad things, or impacts, will happen.

Since many affirmative plans cost money, the link in an argument against such a plan could be simply that the affirmative costs money. Next, you would show that, while the deficit is under control now, the affirmative will cause it to rise. There's evidence that increasing the deficit will cause inflation, maybe another economic depression, and perhaps another world war (impacts). It would be a bad idea to spend all of that money on the affirmative plan now, wouldn't it?

Chapter 6

Putting It All Together

On the day of the debate, always look and act like a professional. Communications research has shown that people make decisions about us within the first 11 to 14 seconds of meeting us, which means that most initial judgment is based on sight. Keep this in mind as you go to your first tournament. Your judge will make certain decisions about you before you ever open your mouth to give your speech. Dress professionally so that your judge will see you as a competent professional. Also, realize that judges and other competitors may hear you when you're in the hallway before and after the debate. Be sure that the things you say won't embarrass you during the round!

You now have the basic building blocks of policy debate. There is much more to know about debate, but you are ready for your first rounds. The last issues you need to understand are flowing, cross-examination, and rebuttals.

Go with the Flow

The policy debate round begins with the reading of the 1AC. While the 1A is reading this speech, the negative team should be writing down what the 1A is saying, specifically the tags, or basic claims, that the affirmative is making. This is called flowing. If you don't take good notes regarding what has already been said, you are likely to miss something important—whether it's an argument they made that you need to answer, or an argument you made that they didn't answer, which is something you will want to point out to the judge.

Flowing requires quick writing and abbreviation. Talk to your coach or another debater about different flowing techniques. Each person develops a style that works for them. Write general notes and tag lines, and learn to speak from those brief things you have written down.

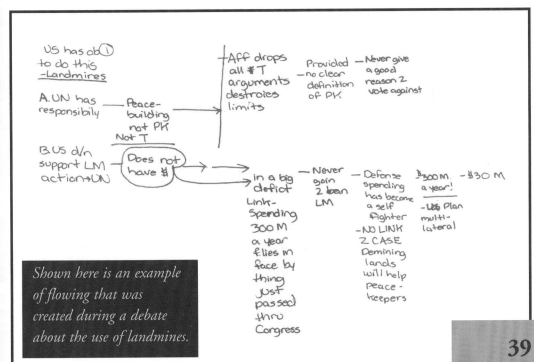

Shown here is an example of flowing that was created during a debate about the use of landmines.

Cross-Examination

Each speaker must be prepared to answer questions at the end of their speech. The person on the opposing team who is not giving the next speech should ask the questions—or cross-examine—so that their colleague can use that time to prepare their speech.

When cross-examining, ask questions about anything you missed during the flowing process. Ask questions about anything that you don't understand or need clarified. You should ask about the evidence they read—what it said specifically, who the author was, and so forth. You should try to ask strategic questions that pin the other team to a specific position. Try to fill all 3 minutes of your time so your partner has time to prepare their speech.

As the constructive speeches progress, each speaker should attempt to respond to the arguments made by the other team in the last speech. Don't reread or repeat evidence unless you are specifically asked to do so by the other team. Read new evidence and make new responses to answer the opposition's arguments. This will make your positions seem more believable. Also, don't just repeat what your colleague said. One strange thing about policy debate is that the second negative constructive (2NC) is followed first by a cross-examination and then by the first negative rebuttal (1NR). If the 2NC simply repeats everything that the 1NC said, then the first negative rebuttalist won't have anything new to talk about. The negative team will be repeating the same argument three times.

Rebuttal

Rebuttals are a time for each side to collapse to their most important arguments and give the judge reasons why their logic, evidence, and argumen-

tation are the better of the two sides. Don't introduce new arguments at this time. Instead, strengthen and extend the arguments you made with constructive speeches. Remember the fort? Constructives are used to build (or construct) the fort; rebuttals are used to make that fort stronger.

As a new debater, you will be tempted to introduce new arguments in rebuttals, if you find a great piece of evidence or a brilliant thought occurs to you after the 2NC. However, you should have made those arguments in the constructive speeches. It simply wouldn't be fair to run new arguments when the negative isn't given time to respond.

You can read more evidence in rebuttals, as long as it supports arguments you already made. You can and should point out contradictions or mistakes in the logic and argumentation of the other team. Finally, you should have a compelling summary for the judge about why they should vote for your team.

Wrap It Up

At the end of the round, shake hands with your opponents. As long as you remember that this is a game and that it's fun to match wits with other debaters, you will truly find this to be one of the most rewarding educational experiences you will ever have. And be sure to thank your judge before you leave the room. There aren't many places in the world where four young people can speak for an hour and a half to an adult without being interrupted! Good luck in your journey through policy debate!

At the end of a competition, trophies are usually awarded to the debate winners. Many winners of local tournaments go on to compete in national tournaments. By the time a debate season is over, national winners have several trophies on display in their homes and schools.

Glossary

clarify To make something clearer by explaining it in greater detail.

constructive An 8-minute speech in which a speaker makes and answers arguments.

contradict To show that something is not true, or that the opposite is true.

cross-examination A 3-minute time period in which the person who has just finished a speech is asked questions by a member of the other team.

defer To put something off until a later time, particularly military service.

deficit The amount by which the money you spend exceeds the money you make.

depression A period during which an economy is greatly affected by unemployment, low production, and poverty.

disarm To give up a supply of weapons or reduce the strength of armed forces.

discrimination The unfair treatment of a person or group because of a prejudice regarding race, ethnic group, age, religion, or gender.

draft An order to join the armed services.

empirical Based on observation and experiment rather than theory.

inflation An increase in the supply of currency in comparison to the availability of goods and services, which results in higher prices.

qualification A skill or trait that makes somebody suitable for a particular job, activity, or task.

quota A maximum quantity that is permitted or needed.

rebuttal A 5-minute speech in which a speaker responds to arguments made by the other team and extends arguments his or her own team has made.

sexism The unfair treatment of a person or group because of a prejudice regarding gender.

testimony Something that supports a fact or a claim.

transition A word, phrase, or passage that links one subject or idea to another in speech or writing.

veto The power of the president to reject the legislation of Congress.

For More Information

American Forensic Association

P.O. Box 256

River Falls, WI 54022-0256

Web site: http://www.americanforensics.org

International Debate Education Association (IDEA)

400 West 59th Street

New York, NY 10019

Phone: (212) 548-0185

Email: webmaster@idebate.org

Web site: http://www.idebate.org

National Forensic League

125 Watson Street

P.O. Box 38

Ripon, WI 54971

Phone: (920) 748-6206

Web site: http://www.nflonline.org

Web Sites

Due to the changing nature of Internet links, the Rosen Publishing Group, Inc., has developed an online list of Web sites related to the subject of this book. This site is updated regularly. Please use this link to access the list: **http://www.rosenlinks.com/psd/pode**

For Further Reading

The Forensic Quarterly. Indianapolis, IN: National Federation of State High School Associations.

Hensley, Dana, and Diana Carlin. *Mastering Competitive Debate*. Lexington, KY: Clark Publishing, 2001.

International Debate Education Association, eds. *The Debatabase Book*. New York: International Debate Education Association, 2004.

Merali, Alim. *Talk the Talk: Speech and Debate Made Easy*. Edmonton, Canada: Gravitas Publishing, 2006.

Phillips, Leslie, William S. Hicks, and Douglas R. Springer. *Basic Debate*. New York: Glencoe/McGraw-Hill, 2001.

Sather, Trevor. *Pros and Cons: A Debaters Handbook*. London, United Kingdom: Routledge, 1999.

Bibliography

Jarman, Jeff. *The Forensic Quarterly* 80, no. 3 (2006).

Miklaszewski, Jim. "Army, Marines Miss Recruiting Goals Again." MSNBC, May 10, 2005. Retrieved July 24, 2006 (http://www.msnbc.msn.com/id/7802712/).

Westheim, Jared S. "Rough Draft." *The Dartmouth Independent*. October 20, 2004. Retrieved July 24, 2006 (http://www.dartmouthindependent.com/archives/2004/10/between_the_lin.html).

Index

About the Author

Cynthia Burgett coaches and teaches at Washburn Rural High School in Topeka, Kansas, where she has been the debate coach since 1986. She holds a B.A. in English and a master's degree in Liberal Arts. In the last decade, she has coached four top ten teams at the National Forensic League national tournament and has been fortunate to work with many talented and successful students at the state level. She lives in Topeka with her mother and her dog.

Photo Credits

Cover © Charles Gupton/Corbis; p. 8 © Getty Images; pp. 11, 19, 27, 30, 31 © Shutterstock; p. 15 © Zave Smith/Corbis; p. 28 © Dennis Degnan/Corbis; pp. 33, 39, 40, 41, 43 courtesy of the National Forensic League.

Editor: Greg Roza
Designer: Haley Wilson